MW00330718

WALK LIKE A MAN

A Path Toward Spiritual Maturity

FIELD THIGPEN

College&Clayton Press

ATHENS, GEORGIA

College&Clayton
Press

Walk Like A Man: A Path Toward Spiritual Maturity
Copyright © 2019 Field Thigpen

College and Clayton Press website:
https://collegeandclayton.com

All fonts used in this book are licensed under the SIL Open
Font License (OFL): https://scripts.sil.org/OFL
EB Garamond: Copyright 2017, The EB Garamond Project.
Linux Libertine: Copyright 2012, Philipp H. Poll.

Cover Design: Daniel Blake Hulsey

ISBN: 978-1-7341915-0-9
Printed in the United States of America

For my dad, Joel,
who has spent my entire life
showing me what a Christian man looks like.

And for my son, T.J.,
who I pray will grow in spiritual maturity and be
even more like Jesus than his father and
grandfather.

Table of Contents

PART FIVE **Along the Journey**

Preface

After being in ministry for over 15 years, I have grown weary of chaos and destruction in men's lives. Divorce, substance abuse, depression, and general instability have wreaked havoc on people I love. While wading into these waters with others, I have noticed two trends. First, men tend to be active in pursuing the things they desire but are passive about spiritual matters. Spirituality may feel like a squishy emotionalism that makes men uncomfortable. They leave spiritual matters to the ladies instead. The result is an epidemic of spiritual weakness. Second, men have a tendency to want to fix broken things. Whatever problems arise, guys want step-by-step actions to fix it. The problem is that sometimes it is not a situation that needs to be fixed, but we ourselves who need to be fixed. This work is not about fixing men, but providing a guide for men to be transformed by the power of God. In *Walk Like A Man*, I attempt to show men that spirituality is not something to be tucked away in a lady's purse, but is a calling to become who we are created to be.

How to Read

I wrote *Walk Like A Man: A Path Toward Spiritual Maturity* in thirty entries, and recommend reading one each day for five days a week. The reading is light, but offers substance to think about through out the day. Like a good cup of coffee, you do not want to guzzle this book.

Sip on it. At a pace of five entries a week, you will have completed the book in six weeks. The entries are undated allowing you the flexibility to read at whatever pace works for your life.

This book could be read individually, or it can be used in a Bible study group, a men's ministry group, or even an informal group of friends from work. If you choose to use *Walk Like A Man* in a group setting, I recommend these three simple steps: (1) Agree to start reading on the same day, (2) Stay on the agreed upon pace, and (3) regularly talk about the readings and discuss ideas you learned, challenges you faced, and encouragements you have taken to heart. Doing so will show that you are not alone in the journey.

Writing Style

When considering the writing style at the outset of this project, I decided to write conversationally. This book is not intended to be a polished, academic work. It is written as we might speak to one another. I want the reader to feel the personal connection of genuine interest and care.

Along that vein, you will not find ten-dollar

theological terms in this book. You will, however, discover the concepts. The reader will encounter doctrines of substitutionary atonement, the *imago Dei,* the imputation of Christ's righteousness, justification, regeneration, sanctification, and others, yet will not encounter such terminology. Theological terminology is important, but I simply sought to engage the theology of the biblical passages without the reader feeling bogged down under the weight of possibly unfamiliar theological jargon. Hopefully, the reader will find the entries light on the eyes and heavy on the soul.

PART ONE
First Step

Day 1:   Seeking a New Satisfaction

"Blessed are those who hunger and thirst for righteousness, for they shall be satisfied."

-Matthew 5:6

More. We always want more. We want more success, more money, more sex, more fun, more rest, more work, more vacation, more respect. We pursue the things we desire, believing happiness will be found in them. We see those who have the things or the life we want and say, "It must be nice."

It's all a daydream. When reality hits, we find ourselves like a dog that finally caught the car it was chasing. When we finally get what we've pursued, we don't know what to do with it and find that what we longed for all along still doesn't satisfy us. King Solomon pursued wealth, women, education, success, and influence. Unlike most of us, he actually achieved it all. He was the picture of our fulfilled desires — except he wasn't happy. He writes in Ecclesiastes 1:2, "Vanity of vanities. All is vanity." Do not let this fact escape you: Solomon had everything you want and pursue, yet his conclusion was that it was still all meaningless. All that you desire brought him no happiness.

It will not bring you happiness either.

It is time for us to stop chasing cars. It is time for us to realize that the pursuits that fill our minds and time will not bring us the fulfillment we want.

It's all wishful thinking with no realistic payoff. The Rolling Stones voiced our frustration when they sang, "I can't get no satisfaction. 'Cause I try and I try and I try and I try . . ."

Jesus has shown us the better way. He has shown us the path to blessedness, happiness, and satisfaction. The better way does not begin with a change of action, but a change of desire.

Men, our desires must be changed. We must hunger and thirst, not for the things of the world, but for righteousness. The desire for righteousness is not common or popular, but it is fulfilling. I hope you are among the men who are ready to stop chasing cars and start pursuing worthwhile, life-bettering, family-strengthening, personally-fulfilling, God-glorifying righteousness. If you are one of these rare men, welcome to the journey.

Lord, I admit I have selfish desires. I am easily tempted by the empty things I value. I want my desires to change but struggle to know how. Help me. I want to desire holiness and godliness, even if I do not yet know exactly how that looks or feels. I don't know what to expect, but know I can not continue chasing cars. Help me to hunger and thirst for righteousness.

Day 2:   Seeking a New Life

*"Then I will sprinkle clean water on you, and you
will be clean; I will cleanse you from all your
filthiness and from all your idols. Moreover, I will
give you a new heart and put a new spirit within
you; and I will remove the heart of stone from your
flesh and give you a new heart of flesh. I will put
My Spirit within you and cause you to walk in My
statutes, and you will be careful to observe My
ordinances."*

-Ezekiel 36:25–27

How many New Year's resolutions have you made
over the years? We have a tendency to start out
with a great ambition for change, but it rarely
works out. Sometimes, a serious situation comes
up in our lives that forces us to look in the mirror
or in the faces of those we love and say, "I am
going to change. I promise." We set out the next
day with the bold determination that this day will
be different. Things will not be the same anymore.
Like a New Year's resolution, these promises often
fade as the days and weeks pass. We find ourselves
sliding back into old habits, back into what we
know to be familiar.

We are chasing cars again.

Many think Christianity is about changing the
way we act, that we are somehow supposed to
muster up enough willpower to stop doing bad
things and start doing good things. If this is true,
then Christianity is about behavior modification

and hardly any different from other world religions. However, the Bible delivers a different message.

God told the people in Ezekiel's day about a coming time when He would make them new. God did not just say they will change for the better, but said they will be made new. He spoke of cleansing them inwardly. The inward cleansing is then shown outwardly by putting away idols. (Do you ever try to put away idols before being inwardly cleansed? It doesn't work very well.) The inward cleansing is accompanied with a new heart and a new spirit.

You will never put away your idols, and you will never stop chasing cars until you are first made new. Your Creator must cleanse you inwardly by giving you a new heart and a new spirit. Quit telling yourself and others you are going to change. Don't settle for change. Seek to be made new.

———————

Lord, in some ways my life seems to be put together, but I am truly broken. Whether others see my brokenness or not, I see it. I pursue idols that promise me happiness but leave me empty. I need to become a new man. I cannot do this on my own. I need You. I need You to make me new. Have mercy on me, Lord. I humbly ask for a new heart, a new spirit, and to be cleansed from the inside out. Thank You for the work You are already doing within me.

Day 3: Seeking a New Direction

"But whatever things were gain to me, those things I have counted as loss for the sake of Christ. More than that, I count all things to be loss in view of the surpassing value of knowing Christ Jesus my Lord, for whom I have suffered the loss of all things, and count them but rubbish so that I may gain Christ, and may be found in Him, not having a righteousness of my own derived from the Law, but that which is through faith in Christ, the righteousness which comes from God on the basis of faith."

-Philippians 3:7–9

"Poop!" I could hear my seven-year-old son yell through the sliding glass door. He had been playing barefooted in the backyard when he found something. I immediately knew he had not found a lost toy, a four-leaf clover, or a hundred-dollar bill. His voice was filled with angst and his face displayed disgust. He raised up his foot to show me what he had found. It really was poop.

My son did not find something good, but something useless and gross. He did not find something worth keeping, but something to be washed away.

Some things in our lives may have the same uselessness as a pile of dung. The Apostle Paul agreed when he wrote the passage above. He said he counted all things as *"skubala* that I may gain Christ." What is *skubala*? It is politely translated as "rubbish" or sometimes as "dung." At its core, *skubala* was a Greek term some might consider as crude. Paul was not mincing his words, but stating exactly what he thought about all the things he once valued. The things he once desired and pursued were now as worthless to him as *skubala* — poop.

You see, it wasn't just that Paul's behavior changed. He changed. Paul changed from the inside out. He was cleansed, made new, given a new heart and spirit by the Lord. Once Paul was made new, his desires began to change. The things he once pursued did not appeal to him the same way anymore. His idols were put away.

Paul did not simply lose interest in the old pursuits. He gained a new one. A new passion took hold of him. His new passion was knowing Christ, gaining Christ, being found in Christ, and having righteousness through faith in Christ. His new relationship with Christ was the basis of his new identity and the direction of his new passion. Being a Christian wasn't a part of his life. It was his life. He says, "To me, to live is Christ" (Philippians 1:21).

You may or may not consider yourself religious, but everyone is religious about something. Everyone pursues something. Will you pursue Christ and find joy in His righteousness, or will you chase something else? Follow Paul's example. Pursue Christ. All the other stuff is *skubala*.

Lord, change the way I think about things. Remove from my heart and mind desires which do not glorify You nor fulfill me. Fill me with a new passion to know Jesus. Help me not to settle for the rubbish in this world I sometimes want or feel like I have to have. As you make me new, set my mind and heart on You.

Day 4:   Seeking a New Identity

"I have been crucified with Christ; and it is no longer I who live, but Christ lives in me; and the life which I now live in the flesh I live by faith in the Son of God, who loved me and gave Himself for me."

-Galatians 2:20

I remember speaking with a young man who was struggling in life. After high school, friends dispersed in different directions. Some went to college. Some went offshore. Some started families. Some went into the military. His friends were all taking their lives in different directions. He felt like he didn't have a direction. He tried this and that but couldn't find his lane. What he did not realize at the time is that the issue was not the uncertainty of his direction, but the uncertainty of his identity. His head was asking, "What should I do?" His soul was asking, "Who am I?"

How do you see yourself? If someone asked you to describe yourself, as awkward as that may be, how would you do it? You may describe your appearance, hair color, or build. You may describe your personality as quiet, friendly, or loud. Chances are, as many men, you describe yourself by what you do. You tell of your skill as a welder, an accountant, or a craftsman. You may find your identity in the roles you fulfill in your home, workplace, and social circles.

If that is you, then you are still searching for who you are. If you see yourself as the life of the party, then what good are you when you are sick? If you see yourself as a painter, then what good are you if your hand is broken? Many men have found themselves at the end of their ropes when their skills and strengths were taken away from them. These men suffer deeply as they feel a loss of significance and wonder, "What am I good for now?" Sadly, too many men have ended their own lives because their sense of identity was destroyed.

So, I ask again: How do you see yourself? Who are you?

In Galatians 2:20, Paul tells us his identity. He described how he saw himself. His identity was not in his own abilities and activities, but was in the cross. Paul looked to the work of Christ on the cross and it was as though he realized, "This is what my life is about. This is me. He loved me and died for me. I will live for Him. This is who I am. My old self has died. I have a new life now, and nothing describes my new life any better than the cross of Jesus Christ."

Lord, help me find who I am in You. Help me to see myself the way You see me. I don't want my life to be defined by my skills, appearance, or personality. I want my life to be shaped and defined by faith in Your crucified Son.

Day 5:   Finding a New Hope

"He made Him who knew no sin to be sin on our behalf, so that we might become the righteousness of God in Him."

-2 *Corinthians 5:21*

Everyone loves a good deal. "Buy, sell, and trade" forums are immensely popular because everyone is looking to find something at a great price. When we give up little and receive a lot, we know we have gotten a good deal.

The Bible teaches that each of us are sinners and owe a penalty, a debt, for our sin. Our sin debt is like a tab we can't afford to pay. No matter how many hours we volunteer in soup kitchens, church functions, or local benefits, we cannot undo our mistakes. We can never go back in time to do it over again. The stain of sin sticks to us, and we can not get rid of it.

Knowing our plight, God sent Jesus into the world to offer us a trade. But before we know what is offered in the trade, we have to realize what Jesus has. He has no sin. His righteousness is perfect. While we are fallen in spiritual debt because of our unrighteousness, Jesus stands as the Son of God in His righteousness. We are poor. He is rich.

While we search for deals that work out in our favor, Jesus extends a deal that works out for the blessing of someone else. His offer is something like this: "Give me the debt of Your sin. I'll pay the price. In exchange, you can have My righteousness and the right to be called a child of God."

It is the most one-sided deal in human history. The Bible says, "For while we were still helpless, at the right time Christ died for the ungodly. For one will hardly die for a righteous man; though perhaps for the good man someone would dare even to die. But God demonstrates His own love toward us, in that while we were yet sinners, Christ died for us" (Romans 5:6–8).

The greatest deal you could ever imagine is on the table. On the cross, Jesus offered His life for you. He died so that you might have spiritual life. Have you taken the deal? Have you exchanged your sin for His righteousness? If so, live in that spiritual freedom. If not, what are you waiting on? Take the trade.

Lord, I look to the cross and realize it should have been me hanging there. Jesus deserved to go free. I deserved the penalty. Thank you for your grace. Thank you for offering me what I do not deserve and could never afford. I trust in Christ as the crucified and risen Savior today and everyday forward. Thank You for taking my sin and giving me Your righteousness. I am undeserving, but I am grateful. Help me now to live with gratitude, love, and devotion to You. Guide me, Lord, to live in righteousness.

Personal Notes

Personal Notes

PART TWO
Next Steps

Day 6: Understanding From the Scriptures

"All Scripture is inspired by God, and is profitable for teaching, for reproof, for rebuke, for correction, and for training in righteousness, that the man of God may be adequate, equipped for every good work."

-2 Timothy 3:16–17

The longest chapter in all the Bible is Psalm 119. Over the course of 176 verses, King David sings a song about the incomparable value of the Lord's Word. He says things like, "Your Word is better to me than thousands of gold and silver pieces," "I love your commandments above gold," and "How sweet are your words to my taste, sweeter than honey to my mouth."

Let's make a confession: Reading the Bible can at times seem more like a job than a joy. Whether battling sleepiness or struggling to comprehend, Bible reading can be challenging. It is all too common to set out with good intentions to read the Bible (maybe a New Year's resolution), start strong, and then soon fizzle out. Many "read through the Bible in a year" plans have gone by the wayside by February when readers hit Leviticus and Numbers.

This was not the case with David. To him, the Scriptures were not a bore nor a burden. Reading the Word of the Lord was not just a religious activity he fulfilled out of duty as though he were working for a gold star next to his name on some heavenly chart. He enjoyed it. He loved it. He treasured it. He repeats over and over again in Psalm 119 that the Lord's words, commandments, statutes, precepts, testimonies, judgments, and laws are the source of his hope and the revival of his spirit.

How can this be? How did David's heart come to love Scripture in this way? The answer is simple. It is not that David understood all of Scripture, but that he understood the value of Scripture. He writes in Psalm 119:105, "Your Word is a lamp to my feet, and a light to my path." You see, David loved Scripture because he realized it is the source of direction and true insight. Living without the Scriptures is like walking through a dark house in the middle of the night. You bump into things. Something is knocked over and broken. You kick your toe, or worse, step on a Lego. Turning on the lights helps us to see the steps which lead to pain and the steps which lead to satisfaction. Regular Bible reading may not always be easy, but the difference it makes in our lives is as illuminating as turning on the light switch.

Lord, "Give me understanding, that I may keep Your Law and observe it with my whole heart. Lead me in Your commandments, for I delight in it. Incline my heart to Your testimonies, and not to selfish gain. Turn my eyes from worthless things; and give me life in Your ways" (Psalm 119:34–37).

Day 7:   Changing Through the Scriptures

"Do not be conformed to this world, but be transformed by the renewal of your mind."

-Romans 12:2

Read over that verse again. Go ahead. I'll wait.

It has a nice ring to it. It's poetic. The writer's thought is stacked with balanced contrasts.
"Do not be ... but be."
"Conformed ... transformed."
"To this world ... by the renewal of your mind."

"Do not be conformed to this world, but be transformed by the renewal of your mind." The words are so smooth, you almost find yourself already memorizing the verse. That is good. It is worth memorizing. This verse should be an ever-present thought in our minds.

You see, the world expects conformity. Our culture and surroundings demand it. From television commercials, to magazines, to radio stations we are being pulled to wear the popular style of jeans, listen to the popular album release, laugh at the popular hit show, and accept the popular opinions of the day. Even those in our society who call the loudest for diversity often expect you to conform to their ideas. They preach acceptance of all views, so long as you agree. Everything around us in this world calls us to conformity. In this society, which preaches diversity, conformity is the real expectation.

Once again, the Bible declares a different message. While the masses may wish to be conformed to this world, we are to be different. Our difference is not born out of arbitrary rebellion. We do not reject the world's ways just because we are cranky or want to be difficult. We reject the world's ways because Scripture has turned on the lights of our minds to see the truth.

The world is still like a dog chasing a car, hoping to find satisfaction in rubbish. Scripture shows us that we do not have to live this way any longer. We can have new life. A new life in Christ, along with a new heart and new spirit, will cultivate within us a new mind. A new way of thinking changes us from the way we once were into something altogether different. It is transformative.

So, would you rather your mind be transformed and changed to be more like Christ, or do you just want to be like everyone else?

Lord, forgive me for the times I cared more about what others thought of me than I did for Your truth. Help me to realize that their approval is empty. Your approval is all that really matters. Help me not to be conformed to this world, but be transformed by the renewal of my mind.

Day 8:   Living By the Scriptures

"How blessed is the man who does not walk in the counsel of the wicked, nor stand in the path of sinners, nor sit in the seat of scoffers! But his delight is in the law of the Lord, and in His law he meditates day and night."

-Psalm 1:1–2

Jesus preached the greatest sermon ever delivered, the Sermon on the Mount found in Matthew 5–7. The ending of his sermon was powerfully clear. He used three illustrations. The first was about two gates. One gate was wide and the path was easy, but it led to destruction. The other gate was narrow and the path was hard, but it led to life. His second illustration was about two trees. The first tree did not bear fruit because it was diseased. The second tree did bear fruit because it was healthy. The final illustration was about the two houses. The first house was built on the sand. When the storm came, it fell. The second house was built on the rock. When the storm came, it stood strong.

All of his closing illustrations were different but pointed to the same truth: Your life will take one of two directions. You will take one gate or the other. You will be one tree or the other. Your life will be one house or the other. You can't do both. You can't be both.

Times come in life when we have to pick a side. You have one attempt at life. This opportunity is too short to spend it straddling a fence. On one hand, we are tempted to say that we want to follow God and do what is right. On the other hand, we are tempted to follow our own selfish desires. We are tempted to want righteousness in one hand and *skubala* in the other. The world tells us this is okay as long as we don't become religious fanatics.

Scripture opens our eyes and transforms our minds to see things as they really are: We can't have it both ways. Our lives will either take one path or the other.

The life that awaits you will either be guided by the ways of the wicked or led by the light of the Lord. One path leads to destruction and the other to blessedness. You will bear good fruit or bad fruit. Your life will weather storms or crumble.

The time has passed to be a spiritual fence-straddler. It is time to choose. Which side are you on?

Lord God, I have seen wickedness, scoffing, and sin. I once enjoyed those things, and am sometimes still tempted by them. But I don't want to desire them anymore. I want to be a righteous man. Have mercy on me. Use the Scriptures to transform my mind. Make me holy, that I might live my life for Your glory.

Day 9:   Overcoming With the Scriptures

"Your word I have hidden in my heart,
That I might not sin against You."

-Psalm 119:11

I know the Pledge of Allegiance. I know exactly what happened when Will Smith whistled for a cab. I know that e=mc² (though I don't understand what it means). I know where Don McLain drove his Chevy. I know my checking account number, the phone number of the restaurant around the corner from my office, the number on my grandparents' old mailbox, and the number of combined Super Bowls won by the New Orleans Saints and Atlanta Falcons.

I did not need to google those things. I know them. Some things just stick with you.

King David was a gifted musician and likely had many songs memorized that he could recall at almost any moment. He realized that being able to recall God's Word when it is needed can be a valuable tool. When reflecting on the value of Scripture, as we have already read in Psalm 119, he writes, "Your Word I have hidden in my heart that I might not sin against You."

If we desire to live in the righteousness of Christ and not according to the ways of the wicked, how can we do it? We know that God's Word is a lamp to our feet and a light to our path, but how does that work in the actual living of our lives? David shares his secret with us all. He hid it in his heart. He read the Scriptures, thought about them, prayed about them, and read them some more. In the process, they began to become ingrained in his mind.

He did not need to google them. He knew them. They just stuck with him.

The result was not a "holier than thou" prideful arrogance. The result was that the Scripture that was tucked away in his heart guarded him from sin and guided him on his path. How does that work? Well, you should try it out.

Identify a temptation in your life that is a struggle for you. Find Bible verses addressing that topic of temptation. Memorize a verse or two that stand out to you. Read them over and over. Work on memorizing them. Write them on an index card to stick in your back pocket and read a few times through the day. Hide it in your heart. Eventually, the troubling temptation will arise again. When it does, the memorized verse will come to the forefront of your mind, encouraging and strengthening you to overcome. If you want to deny sin and live for the Lord, hide His Word in your heart.

Lord, help me treasure Your Word, read it, think on it, pray it, and live it. Lead me, Father.

Day 10: Growing in the Scriptures

"Therefore, putting aside all malice and all deceit and hypocrisy and envy and all slander, like newborn babies, long for the pure milk of the word, so that by it you may grow in respect to salvation."
-1 Peter 2:1–2

Epipotheisate – "long for; desire; yearn for"

I love a good cheeseburger. I enjoy food in general, but there is just something special about a quality cheeseburger. I have had burgers topped with bacon, brisket, mac and cheese, fried pepperjack cheese, fried eggs, fried green tomatoes, fried onions, grilled onions, grilled apple slices, marinara sauce, and even peanut butter and jelly. Each of these was enjoyable in its own way, but it is hard to beat a good old-fashioned traditional cheeseburger. It is my kryptonite. When I haven't had a burger or slab of beef in a few days, the cravings start hitting me hard. I long for it, desire it, and yearn for it.

Peter uses the cravings of a newborn for milk as an illustration for us. Just as the baby yearns for milk, so we should yearn for the Word. (Peter lived a thousand years after David, but they are sounding a lot alike aren't they?) While David expresses his yearning for God's Word, Peter commands us to long for it and then tells us why — "so that by it you may grow in respect to salvation."

Some may see salvation as the end of a spiritual journey. It's as if they say, "Well, I needed to get right with God so I prayed and got baptized. I'm saved now and glad that is settled." In reality though, salvation is the beginning of a journey, not the end. It is not the result of growth, it is the beginning of growth.

Peter says we are to grow in our salvation and that growth is two-fold: longing for the Word and putting sin behind us. A biblical description of sanctification (the proper term for growing in salvation) is "dying to sin and living to righteousness." Both parts are necessary elements. Each supports the other.

Either sin will hinder your righteousness or righteousness will hinder your sin. The two are at war with one another, and your mind is the battlefield. Growing in spiritual maturity necessitates dying to sin and living to righteousness. We will either allow sin to hinder our desire for the Word, or we will allow the Word to hinder our desire for sin.

As much as I might desire cheeseburgers, I had better desire the pure milk of the Word more, otherwise my waist line will be growing faster than my faith.

Lord, strengthen my desire for the truths of Your Word, that I might die to sin and live to righteousness. Help me yearn for holiness so I can grow in salvation.

Personal Notes

Personal Notes

Personal Notes

PART THREE
Following Jesus

Day 11:   His Will for Your Life

"For those whom He foreknew, He also predestined to become conformed to the image of His Son."
-Romans 8:29

"For we are His workmanship, created in Christ Jesus for good works, which God prepared beforehand so that we would walk in them."
-Ephesians 2:10

God has a plan for your life. That plan is often referred to as "His will." Many people have agonized over the question, "What is God's will for my life?" They ask, "God, what is your plan for me?" Thankfully, you never again have to ask that question.

What is God's plan for your life? The Bible tells us pretty plainly in these verses and in numerous others. God's plan for your life is to make you more like Jesus.

Adam was the first created man. He is the first of the human race, the first father of humanity. In Genesis 1:26, Moses tells us that God created Adam in His own image. Just as the moon reflects the light of the sun, so too Adam was created to reflect the glory of the Lord. Unfortunately, Adam sinned, which marred the divine image within him like a cloudy and stained mirror. In an instant, humanity was fallen. We live in this fallen state, not being who we are created to be. Then the Father sent Jesus into the world. The Bible tells us that Jesus is "the radiance of His glory and the exact representation of His nature" (Hebrews 1:3). In other words, Jesus is exactly what Adam failed to be — "the image of the invisible God" (Colossians 1:15).

God's will for your life is to restore His image in you. We know what the image of God looks like. It looks like Jesus. God's plan is to "conform you to the image of His Son." Only then are we able to reflect His glory.

Look at the verses above and notice when God made this plan for your life. He is not making it up as He goes. It has been his plan from the beginning. Before everything, before our creation and the beginning of the world, God's plan for your life was to make you more like Jesus. The purpose of your life is to be like Jesus. You can know the answers when you feel like praying, "God, what do you want me to do? What do you want in my life? What is your plan for me?" God's plan, in any circumstance, is for you to be conformed to the image of Christ.

———————

Father, may Your will be done in my life. I want to be who You created me to be. I want to be more like Jesus. Like a potter molds the clay, I ask you to mold me into the image of Christ.

Day 12:   His Mission for Your Life

"From that time Jesus began to preach and say, 'Repent, for the kingdom of heaven is at hand.' Now as Jesus was walking by the Sea of Galilee, He saw two brothers, Simon who was called Peter, and Andrew his brother, casting a net into the sea; for they were fishermen. And He said to them, 'Follow Me, and I will make you fishers of men.'"

-Matthew 4:17–19

Certain realities demand certain responses. Touching a hot stove will rightfully cause you to snatch your hand away. Hearing a loud boom behind you will cause you to jump. Seeing a stranger drive off with your truck will cause you to call 911. Certain events will bring about certain responses.

Jesus' preaching has a consistent theme: "Repent." Why should we repent? "Because the kingdom of heaven is at hand."

Jesus was fulfilling centuries of Old Testament prophecy about the coming of the Lord to establish His kingdom on the earth. The reality of the Kingdom demanded one response: Repentance. Repentance is both a turning away, and a turning to. One turns away from a previous direction and turns toward the opposite direction. It made sense that Jesus' next command to the first disciples was, "Follow Me." The reality of the Kingdom demands a response of turning away from the current life of sin and turning toward the Lord Jesus to follow Him.

But Jesus' message of "Repent and follow Me" continues with a call to join Him in His mission. He told the fishermen, "I will make you fishers of men." The present Kingdom of God demands we repent from sin and follow Jesus. However, we do not live our new lives following Christ by ourselves. We are to be calling out to others to follow Him with us. The Lord not only deserves our worship, He deserves the worship of others too!

The very next verse after the passage quoted above says, "Immediately, they left their nets and followed Him" (Matthew 4:20). Let me ask you this question: Was there anything else Peter and Andrew should have done? After hearing the message of Jesus, what were they to do? Could they go on living their lives as though nothing had happened?

Certain realities demand certain responses. Once we have heard the message of Jesus Christ, there is only one right response. We are to repent of our sin, follow Him, and share His message with others that they might do the same.

Lord, I have heard your message. There is nothing else I can do. Help me follow You.

Day 13: His Example for Your Life

"[Jesus] got up from supper, and laid aside His garments; and taking a towel, He girded Himself. Then He poured water into the basin and began to wash the disciples' feet and to wipe them with the towel with which He was girded . . . So when He had washed their feet, and taken His garments and reclined at the table again, He said to them, 'Do you know what I have done to you? You call Me Teacher and Lord; and you are right, for so I am. If I then, the Lord and the Teacher, washed your feet, you also ought to wash one another's feet. For I gave you an example that you also should do as I did to you.'"

-John 13:4–5, 12–15

I was once an 18-year-old young man moving to New Orleans to start college. It was only ninety minutes from my small hometown, but culturally, I was worlds away from my familiar slow-paced life. I did not know anyone at school yet, but was confident I would transition to campus life well. I was less confident a couple of days later. As I listened to other students, I heard them talking about the books they were reading, research they were working on, and ideas that were blowing my mind. Within a couple of days, I thought, "I am out of my league. I don't know if I can hang here."

In short time, classes began and the semester was in full swing. I went to the cafeteria for lunch one day. The room was filled with students, campus staff, professors, and administrators all dining together. As I finished and pushed my tray back to talk with new friends, a hand reached over my shoulder and I heard, "May I take this for you?" As I was saying, "Sure, thank you," I looked back to see the man taking my plate to the trash. He was the seminary president. Here I was, feeling like the low man on the totem pole in a strange new city and in a setting that intimidated me, and the big man on campus came and served me. I noticed him for several more minutes walking around the room offering to pick up and throw away finished plates of food. He served students, maintenance workers, professors, office staff, and housekeepers. He served anyone and everyone with a big contagious smile on his face.

Jesus was a leader. He led by serving. When He washed the disciples' feet, He took on a task that was typically the job of the lowest servant on the totem pole. Yet here was Jesus, the King of Glory through whom and for whom all the world was made, doing the job of the lowest man. When Jesus had finished, He taught the disciples to follow His example. For those of us walking the path in life that follows Jesus, we should serve with humility and grace as He has served.

How can you follow His lead? How can you humbly serve others today?

———————————

Father, thank You for the example Jesus has set. Thank you that He would serve us, even offering

Himself as a sacrifice while we were so undeserving. Help me follow His example.

Day 14:   His Suffering for Your Life

"For you have been called for this purpose, since Christ also suffered for you, leaving you an example for you to follow in His steps, 'Who committed no sin, nor was any deceit found in His mouth;' and while being reviled, He did not revile in return; while suffering, He uttered no threats, but kept entrusting Himself to Him who judges righteously; and He Himself bore our sins in His body on the cross, so that we might die to sin and live to righteousness; for by His wounds you were healed. For you were continually straying like sheep, but now you have returned to the Shepherd and Guardian of your souls."

-1 Peter 2:21–25

"That's not fair!"

You may have said that before. I'm sure you have heard someone say it. I know you have at least felt it. We all know the feeling of being slighted. We all know the feeling of being passed over or stepped on without any good reason. We all know the experience of being treated wrongly or paying a price for what someone else did. It is natural for us to be filled with pain, hurt, or anger and exclaim, "That's not fair!"

Injustice is that way. Seeing and experiencing something which should not happen can fill us with all sorts of emotion. Some are healthy. Some are not. Selfishness and bitterness may be crouching at the door. Vengeance may be lurking around the corner.

Do you know what is really unfair, though? An innocent man was once condemned for someone else's crime. He even faced the death penalty for it. Not only that, but he faced the suffering without complaining. He didn't grumble. He didn't whine. He stood up like a man and took on someone else's penalty. He trusted the Heavenly Father to sort it all out.

The innocent man is Jesus. The guilty man is me. "He made Him who knew no sin to be sin on our behalf, so that we might become the righteousness of God in Him" (2 Corinthians 5:21).

God is glorified in our lives not when we angrily declare, "That's not fair," but when we take on suffering with faith that He will sort it all out. When we do this, we become more like Jesus. Others will see your bold faith and may possibly mistake it for weakness. So be it. Life is not always fair. In the Lord Jesus Christ, we don't need it to be. He is enough. He is our strength.

———————

Lord, help me to be like Jesus: To stand up like a man, face suffering, and trust You with all else. This world is filled with turmoil, but You are a God of peace. Help me to trust in Your perfect love, power, and justice.

Day 15: His Compassion for Your Life

"Jesus was going through all the cities and villages, teaching in their synagogues and proclaiming the gospel of the kingdom, and healing every kind of disease and every kind of sickness. Seeing the people, He felt compassion for them, because they were distressed and dispirited like sheep without a shepherd."

-Matthew 9:35–36

Going to Wal-Mart is always an interesting experience. It has nothing to do with the chips and dip selection, the television options, nor the t-shirt varieties. It is the people. Seemingly every type of person in a community is represented at Wal-Mart, a human smorgasbord of culture. People watchers are always treated to a lesson in sociology there.

A sad reality in our world is that while most people share many things in common, it is too easy and too popular to see differences in others and disregard them with disrespect and disinterest. We see someone dressed differently and quietly mumble, "Look at them. What were they thinking?" We hear someone speaking differently and think to ourselves, "They sound ridiculous." We so quickly forget that they are people just like us who are looking for a pack of socks and a loaf of bread.

Jesus also noticed crowds. He passed through areas teaching and healing. People of every color, creed, and class were drawn to Him: religious leaders like Nicodemus, social outcasts like the Samaritan woman, working class Jews like the fishermen, and Roman military officials like the centurion in Luke 7:1-10. These people lived very different lives and represented different social worlds. They were nothing like each other; except they, like we, need the Lord. All of them. Each of them. Jesus' response was not to categorize them, but to love them. He didn't show partiality. He showed compassion. He looked beyond their surface-level social situations and saw deeply into the needs of their souls.

What if we started seeing people that way?

We would be more like Jesus. Being made more like Him will change the way we interact with others. Our Savior has shown us compassion by saving us from our sin. We can't save someone, but we can have compassion for them and point them to the One who can.

Father, help me to learn to do nothing from selfishness or empty conceit, but rather with humility of mind regard others as more important than myself. Help me to not look out merely for my own personal interests, but also for the interests of others (Philippians 2:3–4). Give me the eyes of Jesus, that I might see people and have compassion for them.

Personal Notes

Personal Notes

PART FOUR
Walking in the Spirit

Day 16:   Walking in the Spirit

"But the fruit of the Spirit is love, joy, peace, patience, kindness, goodness, faithfulness, gentleness, self-control; against such things there is no law. Now those who belong to Christ Jesus have crucified the flesh with its passions and desires. If we live by the Spirit, let us also walk by the Spirit."
-Galatians 5:22–25

In Old Testament times, God told the Israelites to construct a tabernacle. It was a tent containing some objects they used in worship, including the sacred Ark of the Covenant. It was a holy place because God was present with Israel in the tabernacle.

Later, Solomon built the Lord a Temple to be His house on earth. The Temple had an inner sanctum called the Holy of Holies. Access was restricted. A large curtain veil separated the inner room from the rest of the Temple. Only certain priests could enter the Holy of Holies at certain times. When priests entered the Holy of Holies, they passed through the veil into the presence of God. The very location of the Holy of Holies was considered to be the place where heaven met earth. God was there.

Both the tabernacle and the Temple reveal to us that sinful man cannot abide in the presence of a holy God. We have no access to God — unless our sin is taken away.

When Jesus died on the cross as a sacrifice for our sin, there was an earthquake. As the city shook, the curtain veil in the Temple tore. Not coincidentally, it tore from top to bottom, signifying that God Himself tore the veil in half. The room, which was a special place filled with God's presence, was now opened up for all. Jesus' death literally tore down the barrier between God and man.

Pentecost was about seven weeks after Jesus' death. Many had gathered to celebrate an annual Jewish Festival, the Feast of Weeks. The earliest Christian believers were filled with the Holy Spirit. The Apostle Paul later taught in his writings that our bodies are now the Temple of the Lord. God's presence is no longer bound by a tent, a Temple, or a holy room. Thanks to Jesus' work of bringing man and God together, God's presence is now found within us!

If the Holy Spirit is present within us, don't you think it will be evident? Don't you think something would be different about us?

The Bible passage above tells us about the Holy Spirit's presence within us. He will "bear fruit," meaning there are certain evidences of His presence. Love, joy, peace, peace, patience, kindness, goodness, faithfulness, gentleness, and self-control are fruits of the Spirit. They are His workings within us, through us, and out of us. Follow His lead and watch Him bear fruit in your life.

Father, please guide me as I strive to live by the Spirit and walk by the Spirit.

Day 17: Walking in Love

"Do not grieve the Holy Spirit of God, by whom you were sealed for the day of redemption. Let all bitterness and wrath and anger and clamor and slander be put away from you, along with all malice. Be kind to one another, tender-hearted, forgiving each other, just as God in Christ also has forgiven you. Therefore be imitators of God, as beloved children; and walk in love, just as Christ also loved you and gave Himself up for us."
-Ephesians 4:30–5:2

A great sorrow in my ministry has been counseling with couples who confess they just don't feel they love each other anymore. It has happened more than I care to count. These relationships often begin with attraction, flutters of the heart, and excitement for a lifetime of happiness together. Financial struggles, sexual tensions, work conflicts, and general relationship stresses threaten to rock their world. They eventually find their way to my office and say, "We just aren't in love anymore."

A great many have missed this truth — Love is not a feeling. Love is an action.

The passage above tells us we should be imitators of God. How can we imitate God? We walk in love. How do we know how to walk in love? We follow Jesus' example. How has Jesus loved us? He gave up His life for us.

Love is not a feeling. Love is an action. Love is a sacrifice.

When you love someone, you love them more than you love the feeling they give you. You desire their well-being above your own. The Bible repeatedly tells us God loves us by showing us He loves us. John 3:16, Romans 5:8, and Ephesians 5:25 each tell us of God's love by pointing us to the cross. I know God loves me, and it has nothing to do with how I feel. In fact, there are some days when I feel selfish, crabby, cranky, insecure, prideful, or any number of other emotions that cloud my judgment. In those times, my emotions will lie to me and cause me to feel things which aren't true. I know God loves me, not because of how I feel, but because of what He has done. He has sacrificed. He has given His own life for mine.

I know God loves me. The cross proves it.

Our challenge now is to follow in Jesus' example. We should walk in the Spirit. We should love others. We should show love through sacrifice. In this, you will bear the fruit of the Spirit.

Father, thank You for Your great love toward me. Thank You for acting out Your love by sending Jesus to die for me even while I was still living sinfully. Help me follow Your example by loving others.

Day 18:   Walking in Joy

"A joyful heart is good medicine,
But a broken spirit dries up the bones."

-Proverbs 17:22

Happiness is a peculiar thing. One minute I am happy when I smell a good hamburger. The next minute I am unhappy when I pay for it. I might remain unhappy while waiting for it longer than I had hoped. Then, I'm happy again after biting into it. The adverse could be true. Perhaps I would be unhappy eating it if after paying for it I realize it is not as good as I had hoped or not worth the money. Traffic is frustrating when I leave, adding to my unhappiness, until a great song comes on the radio and happiness washes over me again.

Happiness is fickle, flipping and flopping in and out of our emotions depending on the moment. Happiness is fleeting, here one minute and gone the next. Happiness is unfaithful, failing to fulfill me when frustrations impose themselves.

Yet, so many build their lives on the unsteady grounds of happiness. When they do so, their lives are as unsteady as the changing tides. Their insecurity is masked by a temporary smile that can only remain propped up by possibly attaining the next selfish pursuit.

Joy, on the other hand, is settled. While happiness is most often dictated by our circumstances, joy is rooted more inwardly. Joy celebrates blessing and endures tribulation. For the believer, joy is rooted in Christ. When we have been rescued from eternal condemnation of our sin because of Jesus' sacrifice, given hope through Christ's Resurrection from the dead, born again as a new person, adopted into the family of God, and filled with the Holy Spirit who sanctifies and guides us, we can have a joy that supersedes all of the temporary things of this world.

The fulfillment that all the world is searching for is found in Christ. They think they are looking for happiness when what they really long for is joy. They want to have a glad heart. They want their spirits lifted when happiness washes in and they want to sustain it when happiness washes out. It is joy. The joy of Christ and of His saving work in our lives is constant through our ups and downs. It is why Paul wrote, "Rejoice in the Lord always; again I will say, rejoice!" (Philippians 4:4). Life will not always be easy. Everything will not always go our way. In fact, some days seem to be stacked against us. Through it all, Jesus has still delivered us from sin and given us an eternal hope. That is unchanging, so rejoice!

Lord, I sometimes feel happy and sometimes feel sad, but help me to always remember what You have done for me and are doing in my life through Christ so my soul will be constant in joy.

Day 19:   Walking in Peace

"Be anxious for nothing, but in everything by prayer and supplication with thanksgiving let your requests be made known to God. And the peace of God, which surpasses all comprehension, will guard your hearts and minds in Christ Jesus . . . for I have learned to be content in whatever circumstances I am. I know how to get along with humble means, and I know how to live in prosperity; in any and every circumstance I have learned the secret of being filled and going hungry, both of having abundance and suffering need."

-Philippians 4:6–7, 11–12

When you stop to think about it, we can get wound up worrying about small things. We easily major on the minors and minor on the majors. We can sometimes make a big deal out of something that really doesn't matter, soon to be forgotten with a short passing of time. While living the daily grind, it can be hard to remind ourselves not to sweat the small stuff.

Sometimes, though, we face a situation that is hardly "small stuff." A panicked phone call, a doctor's diagnosis, an emotional confession, or a pink slip can throw our lives into a chaotic mess of fear, stress, anger, sadness, or depression. Hard times are very real.

Whether dealing with the simple frustrations of a typical day or the major stresses that change our lives, we should remember Jesus' teaching about worry. He teaches us to not worry about our lives and instead trust in the Lord who watches over even the birds of the air and the flowers of the field (Matthew 6:25–33). Paul the Apostle echoes Jesus' teaching by encouraging readers to make their requests known to God through prayer.

Can you imagine living without fear of big problems, anxiety about small matters, and dread for the mundane? There is a word which describes such living: peace.

It is an incredible joy for people who love Jesus to live in peace. Paul described peace in the passage above by writing about his own contentment. He was content, no matter his circumstances. He had peace. It was not dependent on his day or his situations. In fact, he wrote these words from jail. He didn't even deserve to be jailed. The natural reaction is to be filled with anger after being innocently arrested and thrown into a rough jail cell. Paul did not respond this way. He had been born again, was being transformed by the renewal of his mind, and was filled with the peace of the Lord. He didn't have to be angry. He didn't have to be fearful. He didn't have to be stressed. Paul knew the Lord was still in control and he trusted Him fully.

So can you.

Father, strengthen my faith so I can live in peace. I trust You, my Lord and my God.

Day 20: Walking in Patience

"For this finds favor, if for the sake of conscience toward God a person bears up under sorrows when suffering unjustly. For what credit is there if, when you sin and are harshly treated, you endure it with patience? But if when you do what is right and suffer for it you patiently endure it, this finds favor with God."

-1 Peter 2:19–20

Do you consider yourself to be a patient person?

I imagine you are like most people, wishing you had more patience but struggling with the frustrations that bombard us each day. Sometimes our days start with grabbing a cereal box that is empty, looking for car keys that aren't where they are supposed to be, getting held up in traffic because somebody apparently doesn't know how to drive, and arriving to work with an expectation that nothing will go your way today, and it is all downhill from here. We've all been there.

Among the fruits of the Spirit, the evidences of the Holy Spirit filling our lives and transforming us, is the word *makrothumia*. It is often translated as "patience" or sometimes as "long-suffering." We typically think of patience as the opposite of the need for instant gratification. We think of a patient person as someone who can "put up with things pretty well." *Makrothumia* is not exactly like that though. In Greek (the language of the New Testament), *makros* means "far" or "away." *Thumos* means "anger" or "fury." When you put the two parts together, you can see how the word can mean something like "to be far away from anger or fury" and why *makrothumia* was commonly understood as "patience."

So, patience has less to do with not being bothered by the things that come up throughout the day. But it is a virtue of being far away from fury. Paul identifies "outbursts of anger" as one of the "deeds of the flesh," being opposed to the fruits of the Spirit (Galatians 5:20). We will either be a people ready to combust in our hot tempers, or we will be a people who are far from such an outburst.

Peter encourages us toward patience as well. He writes that we ought to be patient with the hardships we bring upon ourselves, but we are blessed even more when we are patient while suffering unjustly. The Holy Spirit enables us to resolve anger as a demonstration of the peace of God reigning in our hearts. This is true patience.

Lord God, I do not want to be a hot-head. I don't want to be filled with anger over little things or even big things. Renew my mind so I can be far away from fury. Mold me into a patient man.

Day 21: Walking in Kindness

"For the one who sows to his own flesh will from the flesh reap corruption, but the one who sows to the Spirit will from the Spirit reap eternal life. Let us not lose heart in doing good, for in due time we will reap if we do not grow weary. So then, while we have opportunity, let us do good to all people, and especially to those who are of the household of the faith."

-Galatians 6:8–10

You have likely heard about karma. How would you describe karma?

Karma is an idea from Eastern religions such as Hinduism and Buddhism. It is sometimes described as "what comes around, goes around," though that is not exactly its religious meaning. In Eastern religions, karma is typically linked with reincarnation. Many believe that if you live a good life, then you will be born into better circumstances in your next life. Adversely, you will be born into a less desirable situation in the next life, possibly even as an animal, if you did not live this life well.

While some religions may teach this, the Bible does not. The Bible teaches about sowing and reaping. The farmer knows what kind of crop he will reap because he knows what kind of seed he has sown. Some actions render natural consequences, and we are not surprised when they unfold in that way.

The Bible does not use the example of sowing and reaping to promise you that everything will go easy in your life as long as you do what is right. By using the contrast of the flesh (our old natural ways of sin before being born again) and the Spirit (our new identity in Christ once we have been born again), the Apostle Paul teaches us that all will reap what is sown according to our actions.

According to karma, we should be kind to one another because it will return a reward for us in the future. According to Christian faith, we should be kind to one another because the Holy Spirit lives within us and is making us more like Jesus. In the first scenario, acts of kindness seek self-benefit. In the second, acts of kindness are a reflection of godliness.

It is obvious which we are to be. We are to be kind not because we are self-seeking, but because we are self-giving like our Savior. In the end, eternal life awaits us. We have eternal hope not because of our own righteousness, but because of Christ's righteousness in us. Let us then "sow to the Spirit" and, like Jesus, be kind.

Lord, You have been so kind to me. You have extended the offer of salvation to me when I least deserved it. Please make me more like Jesus today so I can show your kindness to others.

Day 22:   Walking in Goodness

"To this end also we pray for you always, that our God will count you worthy of your calling, and fulfill every desire for goodness and the work of faith with power, so that the name of our Lord Jesus Christ will be glorified in you, and you in Him, according to the grace of our God and the Lord Jesus Christ."

-2 Thessalonians 1:11-12

You've likely heard the old genie in a lamp scenario. The story starts with someone finding an oil lamp on the ground and a genie comes out when the lamp is rubbed. "I will grant you three wishes," the genie says. Imagine that. Imagine you could have anything in the world. What would you want? Let's be honest, most guys (and maybe even part of ourselves) would want something along the lines of a fortune, a woman, or a private island.

Haven't we chased this car before?

Imagine now you are asked for a wish after your desires have been changed. What might you ask for after you have been made new and transformed by the renewing of your mind? How have your affections, wants, and desires changed?

The Lord God of Heaven and Earth is far greater than any mystical genie. God's divine power is unmatched. His cosmic governance is unparalleled. His perfect goodness is unsurpassed. This

Creator who administers the universe allows us (and desires us!) to bring our requests to Him. We call this prayer. It's as if the Lord says, "What do you desire?"

Paul prays that our Heavenly Father would "fulfill every desire for goodness." The kicker is that we must desire good. This is different from wanting good things to happen to us. Wanting good things to happen to me focuses on self-oriented desires. When we learn to walk in the Spirit, our desires broaden beyond ourselves. We begin to desire the good of others and good in the world around us. The result is "that the name of our Lord Jesus Christ will be glorified in you."

When we walk in the Spirit, the goodness of God will shine through in our lives. It is not so much that we are good, but that He is good and His goodness is evidenced through us. Our flesh may still battle with the desires of worldly things. However, the Holy Spirit is molding us into the image of Christ. The Spirit is teaching us to desire the things that are truly good.

———————————

Heavenly Father, You are good. I still struggle with selfish desires. It is hard, but I can tell You are working on me and changing me. I want to live in a way that displays Your goodness.

Day 23:   Walking in Faithfulness

*"Know therefore that the Lord your God, He is God,
the faithful God, who keeps His covenant and His
lovingkindness to a thousandth generation with
those who love Him and keep His commandments;"*
                                    -Deuteronomy 7:9

*"O love the Lord, all you His godly ones!
The Lord preserves the faithful
And recompenses the proud doer.
Be strong and let your heart take courage,
All you who hope in the Lord."*
                                    -Psalm 31:23–24

Faithfulness is a defining characteristic of the
Lord. It is why He is sometimes referred to as "the
God of Abraham, Isaac, and Jacob." He made
promises to them that He has kept for millennia.
God remembers. He not only remembers in the
sense that His mind does not forget, but He
remembers in a way that leads Him to certain
actions based on past promises. When the Lord
says it, He means it, remembers it, and carries it
through.

Likewise, God's followers are to be faithful. We are
to be faithful to the Lord as we have made a
covenant with Him through the blood of Jesus. We
are to be faithful to our wives as we have made a
covenant with them by the Name of the Lord to be
wed until death. We are to be faithful to keep our
word as people observe us being honest men,
whose "yes is yes" and "no is no."

Those who are being conformed to the image of Christ are being moved by the Holy Spirit, from sinful unfaithfulness toward godly faithfulness. This runs deeper than simply changing our actions. The Lord has changed our identity. He is changing our desires. He is changing our character. We live faithfully only because He molds us to become faithful people.

Are there areas in your life in which you are unfaithful?

God's will is to make you more like Jesus. He is currently changing your character to make you faithful. Make sure monetary and worldly things do not take priority in your life over Him. Make sure your mind is being filled with good things, and not images or thoughts that cause you to see women only for their sexuality. Make sure greed or pride is not leading you to misrepresent the truth. The Holy Spirit is raising us up to be faithful men of integrity who honor the Lord and others in word and in deed.

———————————

Father, thank You for being so faithful. Help me to be faithful like You.

Day 24:   Walking in Gentleness

"Blessed are the gentle, for they shall inherit the earth."

-Matthew 5:5

Who is the manliest man you have ever known? Who do you picture as the portrait of manhood?

Perhaps you think of a fictional character like Captain America, who helps the innocent and battles the bad guys. Maybe you think of someone like the Dwayne "the Rock" Johnson, who has the look and charisma to draw everyone's attention. Maybe you know a real-life war hero as that portrait of manliness. Perhaps you are thinking of a grandfather who worked the farm day in and day out to provide for his family.

Of all the traits we might attribute to manliness, would "gentleness" make the list?

The biblical word often translated as "gentleness" is the same word used at times for "meekness" and "humility." It is the opposite of brashness. When used for a person, it portrays someone who has a quiet strength. Jesus said that such a person is blessed and "shall inherit the earth."

The world confuses meekness for weakness. It is often thought that a gentle or humble person is like a doormat being stepped on by others. "Don't be too gentle, or people will run all over you." Being stepped on, ran over, and disregarded is not exactly the portrait of manliness. But that is not the meaning of meekness.

Jesus showed us what meekness looks like. While here on earth, He had all authority and yet did not show off or step over others. Instead, he valued other people. He served them. He cared for their well-being, even above His own. He spoke strongly of peace. He taught authoritatively of love. He defended the poor and boldly reached out to the outcast while others sneered and mocked.

Some might say that Jesus was too passive, and that got Him killed. Nothing could be farther from the truth. He actively pursued the salvation of His people, and it led Him to the cross. His life was not taken from Him. He laid it down. He was not the victim of evil. He was the victor over evil.

Jesus is the perfect icon of manliness. He is who our heroes should aspire to be. When the love and peace of God take root in our lives, we can live in a calm confidence in the Lord. We relinquish the need to be demanding or brash, and instead can live like Jesus, with gentleness.

———————————

Heavenly Father, I want to be a stronger man. I know that strength doesn't come from within, but from above. Help me to be more strong by being more meek. Please give me a gentle spirit.

Day 25:   Walking in Self-Control

"Everyone who competes in the games exercises self-control in all things. They then do it to receive a perishable wreath, but we an imperishable. Therefore I run in such a way, as not without aim; I box in such a way, as not beating the air; but I discipline my body and make it my slave, so that, after I have preached to others, I myself will not be disqualified."

-1 Corinthians 9:25–27

The Olympics were a big deal in Ancient Greece. Like today, competitors would train over long periods of time in order to prepare themselves for the games. Olympic athletes exhibited tremendous discipline. Winners of the games would receive a wreath to wear as a crown.

Have you ever pursued a goal that required discipline? It is hard work, but worthwhile.

The Apostle Paul occasionally used athletics as an illustration. Just as the athletes exhibit self-control, he likewise disciplined himself. This is the fruit of the Spirit known as "self-control." A man of self-control exercises authority over his flesh. That may sound simple enough, but is actually much more difficult to practice. We might at times set goals for ourselves, and we must be disciplined to achieve them. Whether it is to lose some weight, to wake up earlier in the morning for a new job, or to finish a home project, times come up when we just do not want to do it. It's hard.

We're tired. We don't like it. We want to quit. We want to do something else, anything else, other than what we have to do.

Self-control is the ability to tell our bodies "yes" or "no." We force ourselves to obey. As the passage says, "I discipline my body and make it my slave."

Here is a question worth reflecting upon: Do you control your body, or does your body control you?

Whether we are talking about outbursts of anger, greedy desires, sexual temptations, selfish ambitions, or anything of the sort, we are to be self-controlled. We must make our bodies our slaves. We must not allow our impulses to control our conduct. We are to have power over ourselves.

You will either exercise authority over your desires or your desires will make you a slave. You will either be self-controlled or sin-controlled. Take time to identify undisciplined areas in your life and determine to make that weakness your slave.

————————

Lord God, all authority in heaven and on earth is Yours. Please strengthen me, by Your might, to control myself. Help me in my weakness and I will praise You for the power You have given.

Personal Notes

Personal Notes

Personal Notes

PART FIVE
Along the Journey

Day 26:   Gathering in Fellowship

"And let us consider how to stimulate one another to love and good deeds, not forsaking our own assembling together, as is the habit of some, but encouraging one another; and all the more as you see the day drawing near."

-Hebrews 10:24–25

I once saw a memorable video of a village moving a house. They didn't divide the house. They didn't put it on a trailer. They didn't hook it up to a truck. They picked the house up with their hands and walked it to the new location.

That is not a task for a single person. As the old saying goes, "It takes a village." The people swarmed together, grabbed a hold of the pilings, and worked together. What would have been impossible for one to do alone, the many accomplished as they worked together.

Our American culture is very individualistic. We tend to do things ourselves in our own way and according to our own timetable. This approach to life is often applied to spirituality and religion. The belief is usually, "My religion is my business and your religion is your business." When it comes to spiritual matters, most try to move the house all by themselves.

God's design is not for us to fly solo. He is a God of relationship and created us in His image as people of relationship. The Bible verses above tell us that we should not forsake assembling together. God calls the village together. We are to assemble together so we can accomplish things we could never do ourselves. We are to stimulate one another to love and good deeds. We are to encourage one another. Likewise, we will be stimulated and encouraged.

While we might encounter Bible teachings from television or the internet, we can not manufacture the community of personal relationships without assembling together. It is true that you can spend quality time with the Lord while hunting in the woods, watching Charles Stanley from the couch, or having coffee on your back porch. We can be grateful for such peaceful moments of prayerful reflection. However, the times alone with the Lord are never intended to replace time spent with the Lord among others. We are to worship Him together. Pray for one another. Minister in His Name together. Encourage one another. Lift each other up. Hold one another accountable. We are to assemble together so we can do together those things which we could never do by ourselves. God created us with this need. Knowing this, each of us should strive to gather with other believers for worship, prayer, and ministry — together.

Father, thank You for fellow believers. Forgive me for the ways I sometimes fail to love my neighbor as myself. Bring us together in unity and keep us together, for our good and for Your glory.

Day 27: Living in Worship

"Therefore I urge you, brethren, by the mercies of God, to present your bodies a living and holy sacrifice, acceptable to God, which is your spiritual service of worship."

-Romans 12:1

Have you ever chosen to purchase something you hated to buy? A friend recently lamented buying a new washing machine. He paid money for a new washer. He did not want to do so, but did it because his old one broke. Few people enjoy spending money on replacement parts, taxes, or electricity bills, but choose to do it anyway.

Spending our lives for God in worship should not come with the same sense of dreadful obligation.

I bought a truck several years ago. It was used and in great condition with decent miles. The price was great. I liked it a lot. After a lot of research and assessing the options, I decided to buy it. It was a great deal. Although the price was significantly higher than that of a washing machine, I was glad to spend the money. Years later, I am still glad to have made the purchase knowing that I have definitely gotten my money's worth.

When we realize how great the gift of salvation is, only then do we begin to realize that what we have received from God (spiritual life, forgiveness, purpose, hope, etc.) is worth whatever we have to offer. If the gift of God could be bought with money, we would empty out our wallets, max out our credit cards, and drain our bank accounts. We would shout, "Take my money" in exchange for such a marvelous treasure. This treasure, though, is not bought by money; it is bought by the sacrifice of Jesus' life.

Friends, when you have received the gift of new spiritual life from God, please know the value of what you have. Recognize that it is more valuable than everything you have and everything you are. If you spend your life in service and worship to God, you will not look back with regret. Don't say, "I have to worship God today," with the same lack of enthusiasm as paying taxes. Say, "I get to worship God today," because you know He is infinitely worth whatever you have to offer. Know the joy of giving yourself to Him, living your life as a sacrifice.

Worship Him. Don't just worship Him because it's what you ought to do. Worship Him because it is what you want to do. Worship Him privately and publicly, by yourself and with fellow believers. Worship Him in prayer and song and service and devotion. Worship Him with grateful joy.

———————————

My Lord and God, you are worthy of worship. Thank you for the privilege of even being able to worship You. Cultivate within me a worshipful heart. I praise Your Name and devote my life to You.

Day 28:   Serving in Ministry

*"And all those who had believed were together and
had all things in common; and they began selling
their property and possessions and were sharing
them with all, as anyone might have need."*

-Acts 2:44–45

The Book of Leviticus has a bad reputation with
many people. Those who wish to discredit the
Bible will often point to Leviticus and raise a
complaint. You might ask, "Why is that?" Well,
Leviticus teaches the unpopular truth that sin
leads to death. It pushes the problem of sin front
and center, establishing a system of sacrifice
which ultimately points toward Christ who is the
supreme sacrifice for our sin.

While some try to misuse Leviticus in order to
describe God as some sort of bloodthirsty barbar-
ian, they fail to notice His commands of compassion. For example, God told the harvesters to leave
the corners of the field unharvested. Why? Moses
writes, "You shall leave them for the needy and the
stranger" (Leviticus 19:9–10). It is exactly this type
of arrangement which made provision for Ruth
when she was a poor and needy widow who was
a stranger in the land of God's people. As Israel
was obedient to the command of God, provision
was made for those who were needy.

You may wonder how this truth applies to you
(unless you happen to be a farmer who wants to
leave the corners of the field for the needy). The

early church applied the principle of Leviticus in their fellowship. They understood it was not about the legal requirements of the corners of the field. It was about compassion and ministry. Their response was to meet the needs of others, even when it meant personal sacrifice. Believers were actually selling their personal property so they could get money to give away to others who needed it more!

This is the essence of Jesus' ministry. He gave of Himself for the benefit of others. His example is ours to follow. The early church put their faith to action when faced with need. Notice the words of James: "If a brother or sister is without clothing and in need of daily food, and one of you says to them, 'Go in peace, be warmed and be filled,' and yet you do not give them what is necessary for their body, what use is that?" (James 2:15–16).

The Christian life is a call to put faith into action. Faith, if not accompanied by works, is dead. To follow Christ's example, we must put compassion in action. See others with compassion and minister to them in times of need. After all, is this not what Christ has done for you?

Lord, You are truly a compassionate God. Thank You for the ways You minister to my needs. Help me to follow Your example by being kind and gracious to those I encounter, especially the needy.

Day 29: Sharing in Evangelism

"So Jesus said to them again, 'Peace be with you; as the Father has sent Me, I also send you.'"

-John 20:21

"But you will receive power when the Holy Spirit has come upon you; and you shall be My witnesses both in Jerusalem, and in all Judea and Samaria, and even to the remotest part of the earth."

-Acts 1:8

The word "evangelism" may be intimidating. Statistics show that most believers grow nervous when faced with sharing their faith. However, the passages above demonstrate that evangelism is not an optional part of the Christian life. It is not an unfavorable side dish for us to leave at the buffet line or to slide to the outskirts of our plate. Jesus commanded us to do it. As I might lovingly tell my kids, "I am not asking you to do it. I am telling you." Look at the verses above. Does it look like Jesus is asking?

Jesus did not come to save you and me only. He came to save others too. The Bible teaches us in Romans 10:14–15 that people will never call upon the Lord for salvation until they believe. They will never believe until they hear the message. They will never hear the message until someone tells them.

That is your cue.

Just as the Father sent Jesus into the world to save your soul, Jesus is now sending you to tell others of the salvation He offers. Someone told us. Now we tell others. Evangelism is much more than a good idea. It is God's designed method of reaching humanity. The word itself literally means "to bring good news." Is this not what we do when we tell others about Jesus and how He saved us? We share good news! We do not try to sell them a product or talk them into something they do not want. We simply do what Jesus told us to do — be His witnesses. We tell others what we have seen, heard, and experienced of Christ. We have no need to be intimidated. We simply share good news.

We do not evangelize alone. The Holy Spirit is our Helper. He opens up opportunities. He gives us boldness to speak. He works in the hearts of the hearers. By His power, we tell the Good News of Jesus to those closest to us (our personal Jerusalem), those surrounding us, and even to the uttermost ends of the earth.

A revolution is underway. God is redeeming all kinds of people throughout the world. He is sending you out to do your part. Go and tell somebody.

God, thank you for redemption. I want to share the message with others. I don't always have answers or perfect words, but give me courage to speak up and share the good news of Jesus.

Day 30: Leading in Discipleship

"And Jesus came up and spoke to them saying, 'All authority has been given to Me in heaven and on earth. Go therefore and make disciples of all nations, baptizing them in the name of the Father and the Son and the Holy Spirit, teaching them to observe all that I commanded you; and lo, I am with you always, even to the end of the age.'"
-Matthew 28:18–20

This passage has been famously dubbed "The Great Commission." In Jesus's last words to His disciples before leaving earth, He commissioned them to carry out an order. The order is to make disciples.

A disciple is a follower. The once ragtag group of fishermen, tax collectors, political activists, and blue-collar workers had spent the last three years learning how to follow Jesus. Now, they were being sent out to make more followers.

Imagine if they could have looked down through the future from their time into ours. Do you think these eleven guys could have believed their mission would pass from generation to generation, from continent to continent, and reach us here today? They likely felt overwhelmed by the immense responsibility. (The previous verse actually says they worshipped Jesus but still had some doubts.) They faced an impossible task, but Jesus made it possible.

We have received the faith of those apostles, and we have received the task of those apostles. Jesus leaves us with the same command to make disciples. The mission is daunting, but Jesus gives us what we need for the work.

He gives us motivation and courage. Our motivation is obedient allegiance to the One who has all authority in heaven and on earth. Our courage is steeped in the fact that we are not alone; though we do not see Him, He is with us.

He gives us His strategy. His strategy to spread the Good News throughout the world is to make disciples of all nations by baptizing and teaching. We do not have to come up with a creative gimmick. The plans of the Great Architect work. Our job is to be obedient to His command, share Good News with others that they might believe and be baptized, teach them the truths of God's Word so they will also join the mission of making disciples, and go forth with courage knowing the Lord is with us.

Lord God, I commit myself today to the mission You have given Me. You are teaching me how to follow You. I do not feel worthy or ready, but I am willing to be used by You to lead others. Help me become a disciple-maker.

Personal Notes

Personal Notes

Personal Notes

Scripture Index

Matthew (continued)

Luke

John

Acts

Romans

1 Corinthians

2 Corinthians

Galatians

College&Clayton
Press

A T H E N S ,   G E O R G I A

We are a publishing company dedicated to producing quality works in Christian history, theology, and biblical studies. Our goal is to help foster the love of God with the mind and demonstrate love for others with our actions. Through solid research and biblical interpretation, God transforms us into more open, thoughtful, and generous individuals. Please visit our website for our upcoming titles and other articles explaining more about who we are.

COLLEGEANDCLAYTON.COM

HISTORY // THEOLOGY // BIBLE STUDY

CPSIA information can be obtained
at www.ICGtesting.com
Printed in the USA
FFHW010917141119
56054169-62018FF